BUSY ANIMALS

Learning about Animals in Autumn

by Lisa Bullard illustrated by Nadine Takvorian

PICTURE WINDOW BOOKS
a capstone imprint

Special thanks to our adviser for his expertise:

Terry Flaherty, PhD, Professor of English
Minnesota State University, Mankato

Shelly Lyons, editor; Lori Bye, designer
Nathan Gassman, art director; Jane Klenk, production specialist
The illustrations in this book were created digitally and with pencil.

Picture Window Books
151 Good Counsel Drive
P.O. Box 669
Mankato, MN 56002-0669
877-845-8392
www.capstonepub.com

Printed in the United States of America in North Mankato, Minnesota.
032010 005740CGF10

All books published by Picture Window Books are manufactured with paper containing at least 10 percent post-consumer waste.

Library of Congress Cataloging-in-Publication Data
Bullard, Lisa.
Busy animals : learning about animals in autumn / by Lisa Bullard ; illustrated by Nadine Takvorian.
p. cm. — (Autumn)
Includes index.
ISBN 978-1-4048-6014-8 (library binding)
ISBN 978-1-4048-6389-7 (paperback)
1. Animal behavior—Juvenile literature. 2. Autumn—Juvenile literature. I. Takvorian, Nadine. II. Title. QL751.5.B85 2011
591.5—dc22 2010000902

Summer's warm days have gone.
The air is cool. Autumn has come.
It's chilly today.
Zip up, Laura!
RIVERSIDE NATURE RESERVE

During fall, animals get ready for winter's cold. Rabbits and deer grow thicker fur.

See the rabbit's coat?
It looks as warm as mine!

Animals such as frogs eat a lot in fall. The extra food adds body fat.

Animals live off the fat during winter. That's when meals are hard to find.

Frogs like munching on juicy bugs.
Yuk!

Tree squirrels gather nuts and acorns.
Then they bury or hide the food for winter.

Will the squirrels find their acorns later?

Not all of them. Some acorns will grow into oak trees.

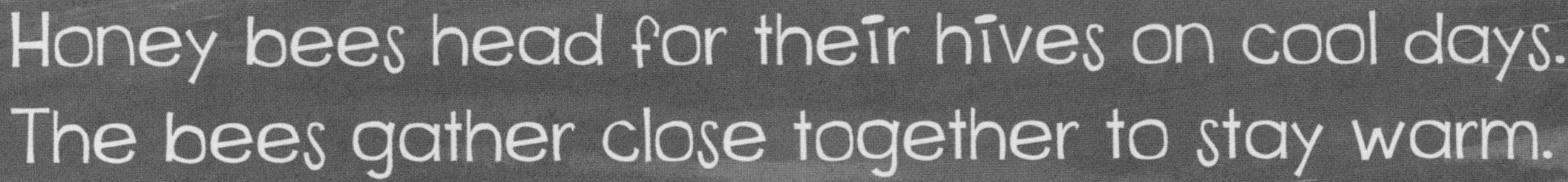

Honey bees head for their hives on cool days. The bees gather close together to stay warm.

Yes. The bees will eat honey during winter.

The hive has honey in it, right?

Beavers build lodges in the water. They use branches and mud to make their homes.

They use those big teeth like saws?
Yes. And they store branches underwater for winter snacks.

Many birds migrate in fall. They fly to warm places where there is plenty of food.

We'll see the birds again next spring.
I wish I could fly to a warmer place for winter!

Many other animals migrate too.

Monarch butterflies travel up to 3,000 miles (4,800 kilometers).

Where do the butterflies go?
Warm places like Mexico and California.

Some animals look for places to hibernate.

Snapping turtles will bury themselves in mud beneath water.

Snapping turtles have strong jaws.
That one doesn't look very happy!

During fall, animals are busy getting ready for winter.

Let's head home. It's getting cold and dark.
And the animals have lots to do!

Make an Easy Bird Feeder

What you need:

- 3-foot-long (1-meter-long) piece of yarn or string
- Empty toilet paper or paper towel tube
- Newspaper
- Butter knife
- Peanut butter or honey
- Wild birdseed (available in bird stores, pet stores, and sometimes in grocery stores)

What you do:

1. Pull the piece of yarn or string through the hole in the tube. Each end of the tube should have a bit of string hanging out.
2. Cover a table with newspaper.
3. Using the butter knife, coat the tube with a thin layer of peanut butter or honey.
4. Spread birdseed on the newspaper. Roll the sticky tube in the birdseed. Tie the yarn or string around the branch of a tree.

Glossary

bury—to hide in the ground

hibernate—to spend winter in a deep sleep

lodge—a beaver's home; beavers use branches and mud to build lodges

migrate—to travel from one place to another when seasons change or food is hard to find

More Books to Read

Graham-Barber, Lynda. *The Animals' Winter Sleep.* Middletown, Del.: Birdsong Books, 2008.

Rustad, Martha E. H. *Animals in Fall.* All about Fall. Mankato, Minn.: Capstone Press, 2008.

Salas, Laura Purdie. *Do Lobsters Leap Waterfalls? A Book About Animal Migration.* Animals All Around. Minneapolis, Minn.: Picture Window Books, 2007.

Internet Sites

FactHound offers a safe, fun way to find Internet sites related to this book. All of the sites on FactHound have been researched by our staff.

Here's all you do:
Visit *www.facthound.com*
FactHound will fetch the best sites for you!

Index

acorns, 8
air, 3
beavers, 12
birds, 14
deer, 4
fat, 6
frogs, 6
fur, 4
hibernation, 18
hives, 10
honey bees, 10
lodges, 12
migration, 14, 16
monarch butterflies, 16
nuts, 8
rabbits, 4
snapping turtles, 18
tree squirrels, 8

Check out all the books in the Autumn series:

Apples, Apples Everywhere!: Learning about Apple Harvests
Busy Animals: Learning about Animals in Autumn
Leaves Fall Down: Learning about Autumn Leaves
Pick a Perfect Pumpkin: Learning about Pumpkin Harvests